For Matt Greco

I am grateful to Sister Margaret Gorman for her research on the stages of spiritual growth in youth; to Père Pierre Babin for his insights on faith; to Frère Charles-Eugene, our host at Taizé; to Père Schmidt, our host at the Abbey of Tamie; and to Phil Pulaski who shared his research on Latin American Youth Ministry with me when I visited Bolivia; to Harvey Cox for his provocative ideas in *The Feast of Fools*; and to my good friend and associate, Peter Ferreira, who is my mentor on adolescence.

Getting in Touch with Jesus

A Spiritual Guide for Young Adults

Joseph Moore

One Liguori Drive
Liguori, Missouri 63057
(314) 464-2500

Imprimi Potest:
Edmund T. Langton, C.SS.R.
Provincial, St. Louis Province
Redemptorist Fathers

Imprimatur:
+ John N. Wurm, S.T.D., Ph. D.
Vicar General, Archdiocese of St. Louis

Printed in U.S.A.
ISBN 0-89243-120-2
Library of Congress Catalog Card Number: 80-81238

All interior photographs by Michael Copek, C.S.C., except for photographs by Wallowitch on pages 24, 72, 89, and 94.

Cover Photo: H. Armstrong Roberts

Table of Contents

Introduction

Get in touch with Jesus; stay in touch with him; really get to know him. This has been the goal of Christians for twenty centuries. And research from the Gallup polls shows that this is the goal of young people today. We may view old realities in new ways. And we definitely have new styles of praying and living the Good News. But Jesus is Number One in our lives.

Still, it isn't easy. Life is more complicated than it used to be. We need more help to sort out where we are coming from and where we are going.

The main thing is our relationships. We can love Jesus only if we love others *as ourselves*. But loving ourselves can be a major problem. We can use all the help we can get.

That is what this book is about. Its focus is our relationships, especially with Jesus. This book not only talks about life with Jesus, it offers ways of actually getting and staying in touch.

So don't just *read* this book. *Work* with it. Use it to deepen your relationships — with yourself, with others, with Jesus Christ. If you really want to, you can get more in touch. He said it himself: *Seek and you will find.*

1 / It Starts with Me

Where Does a Relationship with God Begin?

Some would say it starts in a moment of solitude. Others suggest that it happens only when we have a breathtaking nature experience or when we are so alone and helpless that we cry out for someone.

Situations like these can be settings for getting in touch with God. But they are not the *starting* place. Where it really begins is with my opinion of myself.

Why? Very simple. Jesus has told us that the entire Christian life can be summed up in two ways: "Love God and love your neighbor." Then, from psychology plus experience, we know that if we don't love ourselves we can't love others very well. If I don't love myself I figure that no one else will like me. I'm afraid to get into relationships with others; if anyone discovered the true me I would have no friends at all. I can't let them find out that I am basically no good.

How We Got the Way We Are

We are all this way to some extent, some of us more than others. For some of us, our low self-esteem comes from the way we were treated in our infancy and early childhood. It could also be affected by our place in the family unit, our relationships with other children during early school days, and our general growing-up environment.

There are so many factors that it is hard to say just why a particular person has a poor self-image.

For example, sometimes a person with low self-esteem had a very good childhood. But whatever the causes, not having a good feeling about ourselves, to some degree, seems to be a gut-level experience for everyone.

Ways of Lowering Our Defenses

There are many things we do to hide our low self-esteem. These things are called defense mechanisms. One defense is shyness. Another defense is to act very aloof and independent. Sticking with just one close friend and constantly putting others down are also ways of dealing with personal inferiority.

There are ways to overcome defensive behavior and to grow in self-appreciation. Here are a few possibilities:

- One way is to talk about your self-image with a school counselor or teacher or some other trusted adult.
- It can also help to talk to friends. This can be a help even if all you find out is that you're not the only one with this problem.
- A group retreat can be an excellent experience for gaining a sense of self-worth.
- Another possibility that many people find very helpful is reading. Four good books are:
  - — *Why Am I Afraid to Tell You Who I am?,* by John Powell, S.J.;
  - — *If You Really Knew Me, Would You Still Like Me?,* by Eugene Kennedy;
  - — *Love Yourself,* by Edward Richardson;
  - — *To Love and Be Loved,* by John C. Tormey. (See page 96 for more information on these books.)

Big Ego — Low Self-image

In former times people who wanted to be closer to God were taught to put themselves down. A sample of this approach is the following from a 15th-century book, *The Imitation of Christ*, by Thomas à Kempis:

"But if I humble myself and acknowledge my own nothingness, and cast away all manner of esteem of myself and (as I really am) account myself to be mere dust, your grace will be favorable to me and your light will draw near to my heart" (Book III, Chapter 8).

While *The Imitation of Christ* has many good points, the book is not recommended for young people today. Since the days of Thomas à Kempis, we have developed better ways of understanding our relationship with God. Thomas à Kempis was on target when he said that a "swelled head" or feelings of superiority interfere with spiritual growth. But he was only getting at a defense mechanism, not at the root of the problem. The real issue is that, deep down, people who have an inflated ego really don't think they are worth anything at all. They usually pick one aspect of themselves — their good looks or their skill in some sport or their brains. Then they use that one thing to try to get people to like them or look up to them. If they really felt good and secure about themselves they wouldn't have to brag.

Humility — The Whole Truth

The problem is not that we have too much self-esteem; the problem is that we have too little. The way to become closer to God is not to think worse of yourself but better of yourself, your *whole* self, not just this or that aspect. As Saint Teresa of Avila used to say, "Humility is truth!" To be humble does *not* mean to put yourself down. It does include recognizing your weak points. But most of all, it means *seeing your basic goodness and beauty as a human person created in God's own image*.

Humility means realizing that "God does not make junk." It means taking this fact very seriously — about yourself.

Humility is truth. And the truth about you is: You are living proof that God loves. What brings us closer to God is the humility that says: "Thank you, Lord, for wanting to see yourself reflected in me. Help me to appreciate myself so I can love you more."

The Importance of Intimacy

Another key reason why we need a good self-image is spelled I-N-T-I-M-A-C-Y. Intimacy is the reality we experience when we relate at a deep and meaningful level with one another.

Often a friend or an acquaintance is just waiting for us to share something about ourselves with them, so that he or she can feel free enough to share in return. Somebody has to take the risk first. When we do take the risk, we not only gain a sense of fulfillment, we also give others nourishment for their lives as human persons. To the degree that I open myself up to others, to that degree am I able to open myself up to God.

So, one way to grow in a good self-image (and in a closer relationship with God) is to risk telling others who we are, what we wonder about — our problems, doubts, fears, and hopes.

This is not to say that we should bare our souls to everybody we meet. Risk-taking is for people who have built up a certain level of mutual trust. Most relationships never achieve this level. But it is important to have or to seek at least one close friend who knows you as well as another human being can. In a relationship such as this, your sense of self grows stronger. You begin to value yourself more as you bask in the warmth of human acceptance. Experiencing acceptance, you grow in self-acceptance, which is so important for a relationship of trusting intimacy with God.

Spiritual Exercises

1. Think of the one person you know, apart from family members, who loves you most. Now write: *The main thing this person sees in me that is lovable is . . .*
2. Apart from IQ, appearance, talents, and skills, think of the main quality you see in yourself that is really good. Now write: *Lord, you gave me this reflection of yourself as a personal gift. Thanks for loving me in this way. Please help me to . . .*
3. In chapter 15 of Saint Luke's Gospel, the opponents of Jesus are stern, rigid men, stricter judges than God. In contrast, Jesus reveals a loving Father who is almost too good to be true. Read the story of the wayward or "prodigal" son (Luke 15:11-33), thinking of yourself as that son and of God as your Father who loves you "just the way you are." Then write a brief note: *My dear Father . . .*

2 / Who Is Your God?

What Is Your God Like?

When we were little children we read books that showed pictures of God as a grandfather with a flowing white beard. Artists drew these pictures to give children the idea that God was kind and loving. When it came to portraying Jesus these artists tried to emphasize his great gentleness. That would have been a fine approach, except that, unwittingly, they made a big mistake. Our culture had mistakenly categorized gentleness as primarily a feminine characteristic. (We'll discuss this later in chapter 6.) So, how was Jesus portrayed in these paintings and statues? Oftentimes it was as a namby-pamby, physically delicate man. Nothing could be further from the truth.

Jesus grew up in a small town, lived a simple life, and worked with his hands. He kept himself in good condition. When he was thirty years old he was able to hike up and down his country, over rough, rocky terrain, sleeping outdoors, spending long days responding to crowds, and frequently giving several hours to prayer late at night. He couldn't have done these things unless he had been rugged and physically strong. We must reject these weak images of our Savior because they are not true and can be harmful to us.

God as a Strict Policeman

Another image that can be misinterpreted is the large eye-in-the-triangle picture. It was originally meant to remind Christians of God's ever-present loving providence. That's not the way it has come across to many people. They feel they are being spied upon. Sometimes parents, in their efforts to teach obedience to their children, will reinforce this wrong idea. They will speak about God as someone who sees everything the children do — especially the bad things. In this instance the frightened little children probably do what they are told, but long after the incident they carry around with them this image of God as a severe judge or strict policeman, ready to pounce on them the minute they make a mistake. Even certain Bible stories, taken out of context, can give wrong ideas of God. Children who hear these stories without proper explanations can imagine God as being mean and vindictive and causing all sorts of disasters.

Outgrowing Mistaken Ideas

The first ideas that children have about most things are partial, incomplete, and somewhat inaccurate. But as children grow their ideas are filled out and corrected. But sometimes this development doesn't take place, and then there is trouble — especially if the mistaken notions deal with God, Jesus, or their relationships to us. A person can be a maturing teenager and still think of God as an old man or a fragile person or an avenging policeman. None of these are very appealing images. If that is what we think of God or Jesus no wonder we have no desire to set up relationships with them.

Our first chapter discussed how important it is to have a true image of oneself. If our relationship with God is to be worth anything it is equally important to have a true image of him. As we look into this we realize that some people have another difficulty in thinking about God — it's the question of *where* God is.

Where Is Your God Found?

Talking about God in terms of spatial images poses many problems. Up until modern times people had thought of the sky as a mysterious region. Even with our space probes and our knowledge of astronomy, some of the aura of mystery still clings to the notion of the sky or the heavens — especially when we bring in religious ideas.

Many people, when thinking of Jesus' conception and birth, figure that somehow he came down out of the sky and then was born of Mary at Bethlehem. Then the story of the Ascension at the end of his life can give the impression that at that time he was lifted back up into the sky from which he had come. The problem with this type of thinking is that the sky is a long way off. If God and Jesus are imagined so far away, an important truth can slip away from us. We continue to *believe* that God is everywhere — including here in our midst — but we begin to *feel* that he is a long way off. This leads to other feelings associated with distance. We feel that God is indifferent to us or doesn't understand us or is too occupied with more important matters to care about us.

In Spirit and in Truth

Ever since the beginning of Christianity these ideas about what God is like and where he can be found have received different emphases. In a conversation with the Samaritan woman Jesus told us what he thought was the most important point about a person's worship of God. If our relationship with God is to have real value it must be "in spirit and in truth" (John 4:23).

Down through the centuries sincere believers have tried to discover where this spirit-inspired and truth-filled devotion seemed to work best for them. Each generation had to take up this task anew because situations kept changing. Circumstances were never the same. Certain truths would fade into the background. Others would be rediscovered. The two-thousand-year-old history of this devoted effort would make intriguing reading. The story would run from bloodstained sands of the Roman coliseum to medieval cathedrals, to makeshift jungle altars, to charity hospitals, to silent monastic corridors, to charismatic prayer groups, to young parents teaching their little ones to fold their hands, and, yes, to your old parish church down the street.

Your Grandparents' Generation

It was in that old parish church that your grandparents' generation felt most at home with God. That is what worked best for them. The Latin liturgy's solemnity, dignity, and prayerfulness responded to the longings of their hearts. And their loyalty and steadfastness were rewarded with the graces they would need to survive all the changes they would see in their lifetimes. And now that these changes are taking place, let's not forget nor underestimate the richness of that generation's devotion and how pleasing to God it was.

Finding God in People

Today's youth now have to take up this same task of finding where and how they can best worship and serve God "in spirit and in truth." Like those who have gone before, they are responding to this challenge by rediscovering an old truth: God is to be found in people. This belief has always been present to a certain extent among Christians (including your grandparents' generation), but some have grasped it better than others. It seems to be surfacing again with new intensity.

This insight of seeing God in people has to be a good sign for the modern world, because this doctrine could hardly have better credentials. It's practically a summary of the Gospel message:

Where two or three come together in my name, I am there with them (Matthew 18:20).

As I have loved you, so you must love one another (John 13:34).

I tell you, whenever you did this for one of the least important of these brothers of mine, you did it for me! (Matthew 25:40)

Finding God in the Group

"Finding God in people" oftentimes means "finding God in groups of people." This must be considered another special grace of these times: this awareness of the Lord's presence when two or three are gathered together in his name. When young people experience this almost tangible presence of Christ they don't have to be told what a treasure they are discovering. How could anyone fail to appreciate this pearl of great price?

Who would want to sit on the sidelines during such a treasure hunt? That's why today's youth are so eager to be actively involved in prayer groups, in working together on social action teams, and in participating as fully as possible in liturgical celebrations.

The enthusiasm displayed by those who pray together and share their faith together in this fashion is able to enkindle in all of us a new hope that genuine Christian communities might be possible after all. To grasp what this could mean for the world all we have to do is recall the dramatic effect of the first Christian communities on those who observed them. The early Christian writer Tertullian remarked that even their pagan critics couldn't help noticing how the Christians loved one another so deeply. Their actions were so loving that they gave the impression of being revolutionary. Right now the modern world seems ripe for just such a witness of Christian love.

Finding God in Another Person

This age has also been called "the age of personalism." The appreciation of each person's worth is one of today's values. Surveys have shown that today's young people place the establishing of personal relationships as one of their highest goals. An intense one-to-one relationship — a meeting of two people where defenses are down and the truth and beauty of each is evident — can indeed be another place where God is "felt." It's easy to understand why a feeling of sacredness should accompany every genuine expression of love. The evangelist John puts it this way: "*Dear friends, let us love one another, because love comes from God*" (1 John 4:7).

Finding God in Oneself

Without questioning God's presence in all of creation, people today are also looking within themselves for signs of Divine indwelling. In other words, rather than trying to focus on a distant Creator controlling the universe they are discovering God much closer — deep within themselves. As one spiritual writer put it: "God is closer to you than you are to yourself." Jesus was evidently thinking along these lines when he spoke about the kingdom of God being within us (see Luke 17:21).

The great 16th-century mystic, Saint Teresa of Avila, tells how she became aware of this marvelous presence when she was deep in prayer. Needless to say, the initial discovery thrilled her: "What an incredible privilege — to have the blessed Trinity within oneself!" Then she began to have self-doubts. Had she deceived herself? When she heard that a well-known theologian was passing through town she ran to meet him. She had one question: Was her profound sensing of God-within-herself depicting a reality or not? He reassured her at once. Her experience was valid. He quoted what Jesus had said in the fourth Gospel: "*I will ask the Father, and he will give you another Helper, who will stay with you forever. He is the Spirit, who reveals the truth . . .*" (John 14:16-17) and "*Whoever loves me will obey my teaching. My Father will love him, and my Father and I will come to him and live with him*" (John 14:23). From that time on the presence of God within her was a great consolation to Saint Teresa.

Finding God in the Bible

Another healthy sign of the times is the rediscovery of the Bible. People are reading it and are interested in Biblical topics as never before. What is especially hopeful is that this heightened interest in God's word isn't simply along scholarship lines (important as that is) but is focusing on the Bible as a means of prayer (which is even more important). How an individual or a group can tap into this beautiful method of prayer will be taken up in chapter 4, which is about praying in a personal way.

Spiritual Exercises

1. After returning to earth from outer space, Soviet cosmonauts remarked that they had seen no trace of God in space, which (they said) goes to show that there is no God. Briefly write your own thoughts about the cosmonauts' overly simple view of God.
2. Of all the people you have ever known, who is the most Godlike or Christlike? Write: *The thing about this person that impresses me is her (or his) . . .*
3. Have you ever had an experience that you might describe as an experience of God or of grace? If so, describe it on paper as completely as possible — the time, place, who was there, how you felt, everything about it.

OF TH
CROS
LEAD
HOM
LL THE WAY – JESUS!

3 / Jesus Your Brother

There are other ways to explore who and where God is, and we will discuss some of these in later chapters. But let us say here that God is best revealed in the person of Jesus your Brother.

We learn about Jesus from the Gospels — written records of his basic teachings about life. These New Testament readings relate the activities and sayings of Jesus during his life here on earth. As we read them we should look for a message that cries out to us in our present-day lives. For instance, when Jesus says in Matthew chapter 5 that we should not take revenge on someone who does us wrong, we should examine this general statement and try to see how and where it applies to us as individuals. When he tells us in Matthew chapter 6 not to worry about tomorrow, we should be personally comforted by the idea that God intends to take care of us.

My book called *Good News from Matthew* was written with this purpose in mind. Here is a sample from one of the chapters which will show you how to personalize the Gospel.

Meet Jesus in the Gospels

Once a man came to Jesus. "Teacher," he asked, "what good thing must I do to receive eternal life?"

"Why do you ask me concerning what is good?" answered Jesus. "There is only One who is good. Keep the commandments if you want to enter life."

"What commandments?" he asked.

"Jesus answered, "Do not murder; do not commit adultery; do not steal; do not lie; honor your father and mother; and love your fellow-man as yourself."

"I have obeyed all these commandments," the young man replied. "What else do I need?"

Jesus said to him, "If you want to be perfect, go and sell all you have and give the money to the poor, and you will have riches in heaven; then come and follow me."

When the young man heard this he went away sad, because he was very rich.

Jesus then said to his disciples, "It will be very hard, I tell you, for a rich man to enter the Kingdom of heaven. I tell you something else: it is much harder for a rich man to enter the Kingdom of God than for a camel to go through the eye of a needle" (Matthew 19:19-24).

In case you are wondering how a camel can go through the eye of a needle, some say that the "eye of the needle" alludes to a narrow opening in a wall or between hills of rock. Jesus is referring to the difficulty a camel would have in passing through such an opening.

At first glance, it may appear that Jesus is saying it is wrong to be rich. Upon further study of the New Testament, however, we discover that Jesus does not have anything against the rich; in fact, he even seems to frequent their company. Also, several holy people who have been canonized by the Church as saints (for example, Saint Elizabeth of Hungary) were very wealthy people. In regard to the rich young man: Jesus was sad not because he was rich, but because his wealth was his number one concern. It kept him from putting Jesus first in his life. Is there anything in your life that keeps you from putting Jesus first?

Meet Jesus in the Sacraments

Another way to meet Jesus is in the sacraments of his Church. As youngsters, we learned what a sacrament is: a visible sign of something invisible called grace. We were told that there were seven of them, and we tried to memorize what they could do for us. We saw the Church as a kind of supermarket where we could shop for our spiritual needs. Now, of course, we see them differently; they are divine encounters with Christ, through which we meet more concretely the invisible Spirit of Jesus. They are not things but happenings, which bring and/or increase our personal friendship with God and waken within us our common bond with the People of God.

Baptism

Our first encounter with Christ is at Baptism. Through this sacrament we become adopted sons and daughters of God. Freed from sin by the cleansing waters of Baptism, we become Christians — members of the People of God. But we do not begin our faith journey alone. Baptism is a gift to and from the community. Our priests, parents, godparents, and all the members of the parish have called us to join them. Answering their call, we learn from them what our Catholic faith is all about. Ever grateful for their teaching, we gradually absorb the truths of our faith until we make them our own. Then comes that great moment in our lives when we begin to realize the supreme importance of our faith. And, looking back, we cherish the day of our Baptism.

Reconciliation

It would be praiseworthy if we preserved our baptismal innocence throughout life. But God, who created us with freedom of choice, knows that sometimes we will choose evil instead of good. Because of this, he has provided us with the sacrament of Reconciliation. His Son, Jesus, extends his mercy to us in divine forgiveness. He frees us from the slavery of sin and once more allows us to share his life. This, of course, presumes conversion on our part. We confess our sins not just to get out of trouble but to return (convert) to the God of love whom we have abandoned. Naturally, this will include a heartfelt sorrow for our past lack of love, a firm resolve to avoid falling back again, and a real promise to repair the damage that has been done.

But the question still remains: Why must we confess to a priest? Why don't we just tell God we are sorry and let it go at that? The answer to these questions is that God planned it that way. In the Gospel of John (20:20-23) Jesus commissioned his apostles to forgive sin or refuse to forgive when the person is not properly disposed. (For example, we cannot truthfully say we love God while we still harbor hatred in our hearts.) The priest must therefore know what the sin is before he can advise, counsel, and forgive in the name of Jesus.

Another reason for confessing our sins to a priest is that "confession is good for the soul." We may admit our sins to God in the silence of our hearts, but somehow we feel much better when we verbalize our faults and receive assurance from another that we have been forgiven. And this is the kind of assurance we receive when we confess our sins humbly and sincerely to God's representatives here on earth.

Confirmation

We all received the Holy Spirit at Baptism, but at Confirmation we receive the seal of the Holy Spirit. This means that we are now certified witnesses to Christ. On reaching Christian maturity, we take on new responsibilities. When we receive this sacrament as a teenager we have the opportunity to renew our personal commitment to the faith that we received at Baptism. As witnesses to Christ and proclaimers of his message, we receive special gifts of the Holy Spirit. We all memorized them years ago, but perhaps the most appealing (and necessary) for us today are fortitude and piety. Fortitude — because we need courage to accept our new responsibilities. Piety (better seen as love and loyalty) — because to live a Christian life of service requires loyal love of God and neighbor.

Anointing of the Sick

Whether we look forward to it or not, some day we are going to die. And this being our last encounter with Jesus our Brother here on earth, the Church has a special sacrament for the occasion. Called the Anointing of the Sick, its purpose is to lighten our sufferings (even, at times, to restore our health), forgive our sins, and bring us to eternal salvation. When in danger of death, either from sickness or old age, we should

not delay receiving this sacrament. Anointing provides the opportunity to share more fully in the Cross of Christ and thus prepares us for a fuller share in Christ's Resurrection. As baptized and confirmed young Christians, we have the opportunity of seeking out and caring for the infirm and the aged. The spiritual comfort they receive from this sacrament because we cared will not go unforgotten in the courts of heaven.

Eucharist

Our most profound encounter with Jesus our Brother is in the sacrament of the Eucharist which is made present in the liturgy of the Mass. Jesus is present there, in the person of the priest who celebrates, in the Liturgy of the Word and in the Liturgy of the Eucharist. At the words "This is my Body" and "This is my Blood," he becomes present under the form of bread and wine. And when we receive him at Communion time his presence dwells within our very beings. Mothers are fond of saying to their babies, "I love you so much, I could eat you." Jesus allows us to do just that in the Eucharist.

It is true that many people probably attend Mass out of a sense of duty rather than a desire to show their love for God and to worship with others. This is demonstrated by their lack of involvement both at the Sunday Liturgy and in parish life. There are many reasons for this problem which are not important to explore here. Teenagers are often very sensitive about this matter and are critical of it. Perhaps it would be better to concentrate on the positive and to realize that there are many adults who are truly seeking an experience of community. However, since their generation viewed the Mass almost strictly as personal and individual worship, they find difficulty in changing over to a community experience.

Now this is where teenagers can really help. In many parishes it has been the formation of a folk group by the teens which has made the Liturgy come alive. Young people are now being heard in the Church. The Liturgy requires a community of involved people. Rather than complaining about lack of involvement, youth can bring their unique gifts of vitality and enthusiasm to alter the situation.

Matrimony

In the sacrament of Matrimony we meet Jesus in a very personal way. Christian marriage mirrors the union of Christ with his Church. It is a vocation in and for the Church. Much more than a private arrangement between two people, it is a union which calls for husband and wife to love each other in Christ. They serve each other's most personal needs. They listen to and dialogue with each other, so that their oneness is always alive and growing. And their obvious closeness affects the lives of others — their children and all with whom they come in contact — because of Christ's love in their own hearts. To preserve the beauty of this kind of union a valid Christian marriage is *exclusive* (one man with one woman) and *indissoluble* (only the death of one of the partners can break the bond).

Obviously, the choice of such a state in life demands much thought. A decision to marry is not like choosing the color of the clothes we wish to wear. Marriage is a major decision that should be preceded by consultation with others and by guidance of the Holy Spirit sought through prayer. To drift aimlessly into marriage or to marry because "most of my friends are married" indicates a lack of that very maturity toward which all the sacraments have been leading.

Holy Orders

Not all Catholic young men and women will eventually choose the sacrament of Matrimony as their vocation. Some will remain single for various reasons, one of which could be to better follow their chosen career. Others will remain single and dedicate their lives to the service of God as Brothers or Sisters in a religious Order. Still others (among the men) may choose to receive the sacrament of Holy Orders to serve as diocesan priests or as religious Order priests.

Of course, we all share in the priesthood of Christ. Through Baptism we became members of "a royal priesthood." At Confirmation that designation was strengthened. As members of the priesthood of the faithful, we join with the ministerial priest in the offering of the Eucharist, and we exercise our priesthood by receiving the sacraments and by our witness of a holy life. The ordained priest, however, is chosen to bring about the presence of Christ in the Church and to share in Christ's office as teacher, sanctifier, and leader. He is to preach the Word of God, give pastoral service to the faithful, and celebrate the Mass and the sacraments.

Like the vocation of Matrimony, Holy Orders is

a social sacrament instituted by Christ to insure throughout time the continuation of the Christian community. It, too, demands much thought and preparation before a decision is made. Such a choice cannot be made lightly, because the life of a priest requires that he remain unmarried. But celibacy observed for the sake of the kingdom of heaven (see Matthew 19:12) can be very rewarding. And finally, the decision comes more easily when celibacy is seen not as a sacrifice but as a grace, not as a duty but as a privilege, not as a crucifixion but as a divine blessing.

Meet the Human Jesus

Perhaps it may sound strange to say that we can meet the human Jesus "at play." But this can be a rewarding encounter with him. Unfortunately, our technological society has lost the spirit of play and carefreeness. For the first half of this century reason and the powers of the mind have overshadowed the emotional aspect of our human makeup. This latter has been viewed as a sign of weakness and inferiority. For many centuries Western society has had a distrust of the human body and its capacity for enjoyment. More recently the growing materialism in North America has dulled us to a sense of mystery in life. And teenagers today are victims of all these social influences.

But now a curious phenomenon has emerged. Technology has reduced our need to work so many hours in a day, and we find ourselves with more leisure time than ever before in human history. Our lives have been made easier and our daily chores have been drastically reduced.

Hence we have the opportunity to rediscover a sense of playfulness. Many young people, by the simple fact that they are younger, know better how to play than most adults. The popularity of the Frisbee is a symbol of this healthy attitude.

Jesus, in his human nature, was the model for all free persons. Such people delight in the here and now, realizing that it is impossible to live in either the past or the future. Free persons are confident in the ultimate goodness of life and harbor neither regret nor worry about the future. They realize that because they are human beings many things in life are beyond their control. They consider the human body as a beautiful creation and experience no shame in this regard. They have good self-images and do not worry too much about what other people think. Jesus embodied all these characteristics. He told us that worry is useless and that he came to give us life to the full. He asked us to trust in the Father for our daily bread. He was born into a culture which did not have many hang-ups about the human body.

Youth today by and large have a good sense of the playful. This attitude should be preserved as a real treasure. It should always be remembered, however, that there is a difference between mature and immature playfulness. The former has all of the characteristics we have just discussed. The latter tends to be thoughtless either toward others or oneself or one's environment. So, while it is a wonderful thing to enjoy a good party, it is not playful in our meaning of the word to tank up with beer and go racing in cars. While it is great to appreciate human sexuality and to be unafraid to express warmth in a physical way, it is not truly playful to be very casual about sex. And although it is fun on a picnic to go romping barefoot in the grass, it is not playful to litter the landscape.

To see Jesus as our model of a carefree human spirit, read Luke 9:10-17.

Meet Jesus as a Friend

A final way to meet Jesus is in friendship. We know who God is through looking at his Son, because Jesus is the most perfect revelation of God. When we read about Jesus in the Gospels we can see that he is a very compassionate person always reaching out to other people. Probably the stories of his miracles are the best illustration of this.

Like a true friend, Jesus wants us to be intimate with him. He asks us in John's Gospel to live in him as he lives in us (John 6:56). He also tells us that he wants us to trust him and to ask him for everything we need (John 14:13-14). (We will discuss this in the next chapter.) By giving himself to us as food in the Eucharist, we realize how near he wants to draw to us. He extends himself continually in friendship. How we respond depends on what kind of a friend we are.

There is a famous painting by Holman Hunt which pictures Jesus knocking at a door which has no latch on the outside. According to the artist, the door represents the human heart, and the only latch is on the inside. We ourselves must open it. This illustrates very well the idea that it is up to us to let Jesus enter our lives as a friend.

Listen! I stand at the door and knock; if anyone hears my voice and opens the door, I will come into his house and eat with him, and he will eat with me (Revelation 3:20).

Spiritual Exercises

1. Go to a quiet spot where you can be alone. Now imagine yourself sitting on a beach at sundown. Picture the sea and the sky. Listen to the waves. Now, notice someone in a long, white tunic walking toward you. He has long hair and a beard. His name is Jesus. When he is standing next to you, look up at his face and study it. Invite him to sit down beside you. Now share with him what is on your mind at this moment.

2. In his early life, Saint Paul (who was known then as Saul) used to capture Christians and put them in prison. When he had his famous conversion experience, he heard a voice saying, *Saul, Saul, why do you persecute ME?* Saul said: *Who are you, Lord?* The voice said: *I am JESUS, whom you are persecuting.*

   Answer in writing:
   - Why did Jesus say that Paul was persecuting Jesus himself when he persecuted Christians?
   - What do Jesus' words to Paul tell you about *where* Jesus is alive today?

3. When you receive Holy Communion, the priest says "The body of Christ," and you say "Amen." Saint Augustine tells us that "body of Christ" means Jesus' *risen* body, his body the *Church,* and his *Eucharistic* body. And your *Amen* means: "Yes, *we are* the body of Christ." What does this tell you about *where* Jesus is?

4 / How to Pray in a Personal Way

Teenagers today have a real thirst for religious experience. Of the 25 million teenagers in the United States, eight million are involved in Bible study groups. Another seven million pursue various activities that give them a deep sense of God. Nine out of ten young Americans pray. Four out of ten pray frequently. According to any standards, American teenagers are highly religious.

The Meaning Behind the Words

Part of the young person's sincere religious effort is the desire to understand the reason behind things. As one example, obedience makes more sense when the reasons behind certain regulations are made clear.

This quest for meaning also applies to prayer. Most young people don't like rote recitation. They are critical of those others who loudly mouth the traditional prayers but apparently do not consider the meaning behind the words they are saying. Maybe a person will shy away from the prayer experience because of the mistaken notion that such "praying" is true prayer. It isn't, and it is good to know that there's a perfectly valid and worthwhile way of praying that is nothing like that. It's always possible to talk to God or to Jesus in one's own way from one's own heart. In fact, it would be hard to beat that prayer.

Prayer and Our Moods

God wants us to speak to him from where we are right now. Moods are not to be ignored. If a person is mad or sad, depressed or frustrated, then that's the way he should present himself to God. If someone feels the need for help, then that person should ask the Lord for it. If a blessing has come to someone, then thankfulness should be expressed. We don't have to try to get ourselves into a "holy" frame of mind. God accepts us as we are — even when we are in our darkest moods.

Another point to remember about praying is that longer doesn't necessarily equal better. It's much more important to be genuine. There are other aspects to this prayer-time relationship, and these will be discussed in the next chapter.

There's also considerable leeway in deciding where the best place for prayer might be. Some pray better outdoors in nature. Some like it quiet, while others prefer background music. Some like to pray alone and in privacy. Others find strength and inspiration in group settings. It sounds like a paradox, but experience has shown that even in a large group a person's prayer can still become quite personal.

Praying in Groups

Should an opportunity present itself to attend a prayer meeting, take it. What will it be like? The people will sing songs together. They will reverently listen to readings from Scripture. There will be quiet times. After awhile, someone will speak out in spontaneous prayer. Several others might do the same. Someone will begin a familiar song or improvise on an old song or even a new one. Two or three people will witness to what God has been doing in their lives.

Besides these external expressions of prayer, what else will be experienced? Chances are you will detect an atmosphere of peace and tranquillity along with an almost irrepressible joyfulness. Be warned: The above are catching!

The Prayer of Petition

The prayer of petition is based on Jesus' words in Luke's Gospel: *And so I say to you: Ask, and you will receive; seek, and you will find; knock, and the door will be opened to you* (Luke 11:9). Many other Gospel passages speak about this type of prayer and what goes into it. Some of the parables are centered around this theme. In all the stories the underlying assumption is: God cares for us. He hears us when we turn to him for help. If human beings respond to pleas for help (in the parables even unjust judges, irritable neighbors, and worldly businessmen respond) surely God who is our loving Father will give us what is best for us.

Other Considerations

Here are some other considerations to bear in mind when you are asking God for things in prayer.

- Ordinarily God does not reverse the course of nature which is already set in motion.
- When we pray, we must be experiencing a genuine need. God is not going to give us every passing fancy we come across.

- Human effort must accompany prayer for the same objective. God will not give me a high grade on a test if I never bother to study. "The Lord helps those who help themselves."
- In addition to faith, Jesus demands persistence. Read Luke 11:5-8 about the importunate friend.
- Sometimes, because God's reasons aren't our own, certain prayers seem to remain unanswered (that's because we are looking at it from our own perspective).
- Lastly, it is important to realize that we are not mere puppets here on earth. God has given us the wonderful ability to make choices. Most of the time we can create our own "divine providence" by being faithful to all that is best within us and by acting accordingly.

Trusting Prayer

Praying the prayer of petition and trusting in God go hand in hand. When they do, life can be like a spiritual adventure. It can be like flying in an airplane without knowing the destination but all the while trusting that it will land in a safe place. To enter into this kind of trusting prayer is to be swept into the profound awareness that God is with me at all times and in all situations. I don't have to be afraid of anything, not even death. This kind of general awareness of God's ever-present concern for me is much more comforting than always being concerned about concrete results from this or that request.

Meditation

Meditation is another kind of prayer. It's a special way of thinking about something. We use not only our minds but we also turn the spotlight of faith on the topic. We can meditate by reviewing a good insight, by recalling all the situations in which God has helped us during our life, or by expanding on an idea that we got when we were in prayer. One of the best ways to meditate is to use a book and to keep the written word in front of us. This method helps us to focus our attention. Perhaps we can keep our thoughts from straying too far. Reading slowly, pausing frequently to talk to God, asking for help — all this can lead to important graces. For meditation you can use just about any book of prayers, poems, or inspirational readings, as long as it really moves you to talk to God.

Praying the Gospels

The best book for meditation would have to be the Bible. Since that is really a collection of many books, we can make a further choice. That would take us into the New Testament, and among those the preference (especially for beginners) would have to be for the four Gospels. Any one of these Gospels would prove to be excellent meditation material because the words of Jesus are always living. They were spoken for and to us, as well as to the people of those days. Also, unlike other books, the words of the Gospel can never be exhausted. We can always discover new and deeper meanings in what Jesus said.

Meditating a Gospel Scene

Let's run through a sample Gospel meditation to see how it can be done. Open your Bible to Mark 4:35-51. Read it over slowly and then let your imagination fill in the details. It is evening, and you are standing in a crowd on the shore of the Sea of Galilee. Jesus is in a boat about to be launched. He wants to go to the other side. Imagine yourself pushing the boat off the sand and then jumping into it along with some of the disciples. The Master is very tired, so he goes to the stern to get some rest. Soon he falls asleep. Meanwhile, the wind has picked up. The waves are getting choppier. Even the experienced fishermen are concerned. The boat is shipping water — yet Jesus sleeps on. If the storm gets worse, you will all go down. You and some of the disciples wake Jesus with the words, "Teacher, does it not matter to you that we are going to drown?" Jesus stands up and tells the wind to be quiet and the waves to still. And that's what happens. The lake is as smooth as glass, and only the gentlest of breezes touches your cheeks. He turns and looks at you. "Why did you have so little faith?"

What did you feel like when Jesus asked you that? Why don't you trust him more in your life? He will be Savior for each one of us right now — if we only let him.

Mark, Matthew, Luke, and John

Marilyn Norquist has written a very helpful booklet entitled *How to Read and Pray the Gospels* (Liguori Publications; for more information, see page 96). The author offers a number of useful prayer techniques for each Gospel. For Mark, besides the scene-creating method just used, she also suggests a personal dialogue flowing out of one of the stories. She says: "Speak to Jesus directly. See him turn to you and answer. Listen to him . . . ."

According to Ms. Norquist, prayer with Matthew is active prayer. Begin with petitions and inner attitudes. Examine the motives behind your actions. Place these next to the Gospel motives. The second kind of prayer in Matthew is behavioral prayer. Play "follow the leader" behind Christ. For example, in Matthew 7:1-2, what does Jesus say about judging others? Most of us have a critical streak within us. If we keep Jesus' words and example ever before us we might be able to steer clear of those "put-downs" we are tempted to make.

If we pray Luke's Gospel with sincerity we can grow in receptivity. We can become fine-tuned to what God is asking of us. This would lead to another type of prayer that flows out of Luke's style: the prayer of praise. Read Luke 1:46-55 or 1:68-79. Search the Gospel for all its joyful words, such as *rejoice, blessed, exalt, exult, happy*.

John's Gospel is different from the first three. Its tone is elevated and poetic. It teaches the highest level of theology. Yet, despite the sublimity of its doctrine and style, its appeal is almost universal. Somehow it touches our hearts like nothing else. It's a "natural" for leading into contemplative prayer.

Contemplative Prayer

What is contemplative prayer? Contemplation is not quite the same as meditation, although sometimes the words are used interchangeably. When people talk about transcendental meditation and Eastern meditation they are really talking about something that is more like contemplation. In contemplation there is an effort to suspend the thought process. So the stress is not on thinking but on letting go of thoughts. We try to quiet ourselves down. In this style of prayer we're not trying to imagine scenes or to take part in dialogues. In fact, it's not so much a question of speaking to God as of being absorbed in silence and letting God speak to you.

In our human relationships it's important to know how to listen. The same is true with regard to our relationship to God. In contemplative prayer we try to dampen all the static of our lives so we can listen to what God is telling us about himself. That is why contemplation is defined as "the awareness of God, known and loved at the core of one's being" (from *Contemplative Prayer,* by Father James Borst; see page 96 for more information). And that is why contemplation is one of the best forms of prayer. It is not surprising that people who contemplate for several hours a day tend to be very peaceful people who seem very close to God.

Questions About Contemplative Prayer

- Where to pray? Preferably where you can be alone — any place where you are unlikely to be disturbed.
- How long to pray? For a beginner, start with five minutes a day of quieting yourself down. Work up to twenty minutes or a half hour of prayer. Beyond that, seek advice about this from someone who is skilled in this type of prayer.
- When to pray? It depends on what your

circumstances allow and what works best for you. Once this is decided, try to be faithful to it.

- What posture is best? "Comfortable, but not too comfortable" is the usual answer. Don't slouch, and keep your backbone straight — a restful but alert position. Good body tone is important. A rhythmic breathing pattern can be helpful.

  (See *Yoga for Young Children,* by Esther-Martina Luchs. Fuller information can be found on page 96.)

- What about repeated prayers? Having a word or phrase on which to focus is recommended. Jesus used "Abba" as his centering prayer. You can choose the sacred name itself or some phrase like "My Jesus, mercy." The famous Jesus Prayer is, "Jesus, Son of the living God, have mercy on me a sinner." You can also repeat part of the Lord's Prayer in the same manner. The point is, use whatever word or phrase helps you to get into and to remain in contact with the Father, Son, and Holy Spirit dwelling within you.

The Rosary

Some young people have rediscovered the rosary. This very old and revered devotion has the potential of providing all the above types of prayer. It is filled with petitions. Its fifteen mysteries are scriptural meditations of a high order. And its repetition of key phrases and its centering on Jesus can be conducive to deep contemplative prayer. Don't underestimate the richness of the rosary.

Spiritual Direction

This chapter in and of itself may not be sufficient for some of you to begin to pray on your own. Many of us need what is called "spiritual direction."

Spiritual direction means that one person who is more experienced in prayer helps another person or group of persons less experienced in prayer. If you are serious about praying you should think about asking some trusted adult to do this for you. He or she doesn't have to be someone who is in church all the time. Rather, that someone should be a person in whom you can sense a real faith and trust in Jesus, someone who has integrated religion into normal human life. It could be helpful to spend a half hour or so with that person once a week or once a month or whatever seems best to both of you.

The subject of your conversations would be your prayer — how well or how poorly you have been doing in your efforts to try some of the methods mentioned above. Because your older friend has had experience at prayer, he or she will be able to give you much practical guidance.

A Prayer Journal

One recommendation might be to keep a prayer journal. This is simply a notebook where either daily or occasionally you take a few minutes to jot down thoughts that you received in prayer or questions that might have come up. The journal can help both you and your director in noticing patterns in your life with God.

Spiritual Exercises

1. Turn to "Meditating a Gospel Scene" on page 44. Do the meditation described there. Then write a brief note to Jesus: *Dear Lord, during the meditation, this is what I thought and felt . . .*
2. In this chapter three good and fairly inexpensive books on prayer are recommended. (See pages 45, 47, and 49.) Go to a religious bookstore — or to your school librarian — and order one of these books. Make a resolution to read the book cover to cover and to do what it suggests.
3. Give serious consideration to the suggestion offered in the section "Spiritual Direction" on page 50. Write down the name(s) of one or two persons you might like for a spiritual director and pick a day when you will talk to one of them about it.

5 / Going with the Jesus Flow

Getting a true understanding of yourself, discovering God in your prayers, sensing the Lord's presence when you're with others, meeting him face-to-face in the sacraments, listening to him speak to you from the Bible — all this sounds great. It's exactly what most young people have been searching for. But in real life it doesn't seem to happen that way, at least not very easily. Why not? What's the big problem? What could be holding a person back from really praying?

The Number One Obstacle

It's true that teenagers, like their elders, face a stiff obstacle in their search for deeper prayer. The name of that obstacle is The Fast Pace of Life.

Let's look at just one aspect — the "instant" side of American life:

We have "instant" coffee and "fast" food. (The food may not always be hot, but it is fast.)

Thanks to "plastic money" we have instant cash and instant credit.

Thanks to Ma Bell we have instant communications. Soon we'll even be able to see each other face-to-face on a video screen while we talk long-distance.

Rapid communications and services expand our lives in ways people 50 years ago never dreamed of. But there is a personal price we pay for all this "instant" living. *It tends to make us very short on patience.*

Human Relationships

One of the key problems flowing from our instant life-style is spelled D-E-L-U-S-I-O-N. Instant living creates the delusion that everything in life can happen right now — including human relationships.

That, of course, is a Class A delusion. All of us who have grown into a good friendship are aware of that fact. But there are some people who are not aware of it. That is why, for example, some people try to achieve "instant intimacy" by rushing into a sexual relationship with another person. Sexual *contact* can be something quick and easy. But sexual *intimacy* — a relationship with genuine human feeling and real caring — does not happen that way. "Close encounters of the instant kind" seldom lead anywhere — except, too often, in the direction of depression, hurt, and loss of trust.

Relationship with Jesus

Human relationships need to grow. The same thing is true of a relationship with Jesus. Many young people are seeking a relationship with him. But what some are finding is The Obstacle. As George Harrison sings in "My Sweet Lord": "I really want to see you . . . I really want to feel you . . . *but it takes so long,* my Lord."

Intimacy with Jesus needs to grow. Some people have tried to find a shortcut to spiritual intimacy, using pot and other drugs. This is the "plant food" theory. Give the organism a shot of chemical nutrients and it grows twice as fast. This technique works wonders — for plants. But if you turn yourself into a "potted plant," the spiritual experience you have is not an intimate relationship with Jesus.

There definitely is such a thing as a genuine "spiritual high." People experience these highs in all kinds of situations: seeing a sunset, reading a book, watching your baby come into the world. But there are also "spiritual" highs that are a delusion.

What is the difference between the two? One difference is this: A genuine spiritual high never ends in depression when you "come down." It has just the opposite effect: It leaves you with a desire for deeper intimacy with the Lord. When the high is genuine, what you want afterwards is the Lord. When the high is a delusion, what you want afterwards is another high.

A good norm to use in this matter is the Gamaliel Principle. In Acts of the Apostles, the high priests in Jerusalem wondered what to think about a new group that worshiped an executed criminal, Jesus of Nazareth. Rabbi Gamaliel stood up in the assembly and gave his peers perfect advice. He said: *If what they have planned and done is of human origin, it will disappear, but if it comes from God, you cannot possibly defeat them* (Acts 5:38-39).

Use the Gamaliel Principle. If you experience a spiritual high that is not "man-made," one that opens you up to God, let it make a real difference in your life. Spiritual highs can make us highly spiritual if we let them lead us to the Lord.

The Price We End Up Paying

There is an old expression: "Time is money." Industry lives by that axiom. Business establish-

ments constantly search for ways to produce more goods in less time. It is a way of life with us.

To a great extent, this tendency comes from the centuries-old view that work is good and rest is evil — "Idle hands are the devil's workshop." Pushed beyond its limits, this mentality is pressuring young people to achieve, achieve, achieve almost from the moment they are born.

A number of problems flow from this tendency. For one thing, it draws people away from looking within. For a person with low self-esteem, achieving and getting "results" is an escape hatch. As long as a person is on the move and "where the action is," there is no need to face and deal with the deep feeling that "I'm not worth much." Thanks to the drive to "become somebody," many Americans live their whole lives feeling deep down that they are nothing but a piece of junk.

Another problem that flows from "Keep it moving, baby" is family breakdown. Family members are together less and less as time goes on. As a result, many family members don't *feel* like "family" to each other. A relaxed supper at home seems like a waste of good time. Why spend an hour eating with our family when we could be out where the action is? The bottom line reads: Families are falling apart because they are never together.

Then there is the problem with prayer. "I really want to see you, Lord — but I can't find the time." "I really want to feel you, Lord — but I'm too caught up in the fast pace of life to relax and just BE with you." "I'd like to get to know you,

Lord — but it takes so long, and I've got too much to DO."

The Choice Is Ours

American teenagers are highly religious. They have a real thirst for religious experience. The question is: Are they going to go along with the social pressure that produces unfulfilled persons, shallow relationships, and spiritual undernourishment?

None of us *has* to go along with that flow. We can go with the other one.

We can live by the old Moslem proverb: "Don't *do* anything before you stand there."

We can turn off the radio and let the silent voice of God come through.

We can scale down our minds racing ahead to "what's happening next" and appreciate a friend, talk with a grandparent, take a hike in the woods, sit on the porch and just let the universe sink into the pores of our consciousness.

We can make family meals *real* meals. And at the Eucharist, we can learn to focus on Jesus, so that we catch the depth of Saint Paul's words: *Because there is the one loaf of bread, all of us, though many, are one body, for we all share the same loaf* (1 Corinthians 10:17).

We can do these things — hundreds of things that "instant living" deprives us of. Instant living has its points. But so do caring relationships, really knowing Jesus, and *being one with each other* in him. When you look at the two flows side by side, it makes you wonder why we ever let ourselves get sucked into the Fast Pace of Life.

Spiritual Exercises

1. Think back over the past week. Recall a time when you were frustrated because something was delayed or didn't turn out right. Write: *I felt frustrated by what happened because of my tendency to . . .*

2. Being *close* to your family depends a lot on being *with* your family. Write:
   - The one person in my family I could be much closer to if we spent more time together is . . .
   - The reason I don't spend more time with him/her is because . . .
   - From now on I plan to . . . (Be as definite as possible about time and place.)

3. Being *close* to Jesus depends a lot on being *with* Jesus. Write:
   - The reason I don't spend more time with Jesus is because . . .
   - From now on I plan to . . . (Be as definite as possible about time and place.)

ROCKY

6 / Today's Challenges

There's an old song that has a line like this in it: "You've gotta accentuate the positive; eliminate the negative; latch on to the affirmative; and don't mess with Mr. In-between." This chapter is going to proceed in that direction. In other words, rather than talking about sin or what can go wrong in a person's life, we would prefer to discuss the challenges to growth and to goodness that are offered to young people today.

One of the challenges is to acquire sufficient wisdom so as not to be taken in by some current misconceptions. One such misconception is that certain ideas always have to be linked together — that you can't have one without the other. One set of examples: strength and masculinity, weakness and femininity.

Strength and Weakness

It's true that as a group men are physically stronger than women. They can run faster, jump higher, and lift heavier loads. Even so, there's recent evidence that women are better at enduring pain, have more patience, and can handle extended difficulties better than men. In any case, the quality of true strength is not to be measured merely by the size of one's muscles but by the whole person's reaction to stress or an obstacle. How much courage can be summoned up? How much dedication to an important cause can be found within the person? When we ask these broader questions we see that strength or weakness should not be linked exclusively to either sex.

Thinking and Feeling

Another set of linkages that isn't very good is this one: logical thinking and control (men), emotional display and inconsistency (women). These generalizations simply aren't true. Women are just as capable of rigorous logic and keen analytical thought as men. Nor is it true that being able to think reasonably is better than being in tune with one's feelings. These are two completely different processes and should not be compared in this way.

Both sexes have suffered because of this linkage. Women have been deprived of jobs and easy access into certain professions because of this. Many men simply don't know what to do with their emotions. As a consequence, they are emotionally starved. When they were very little they were told, "Boys do not cry!" This has remained with them and (with the exception of anger) they consider any emotional expression as weakness. This can lead to cruelty, hardness of heart, and self-centeredness.

Being "Macho"

"Macho" is the symbol of this distorted view of manliness. Many teenage boys feel that they have to be "macho" in order to get peer acceptance. Others feel threatened by their own search for a sexual identity, particularly if they have ever had even a fleeting homosexual feeling. (Homosexual feelings are not at all abnormal during adolescence and do not mean that a person is a homosexual.) Most often the "macho" image is a defense mechanism coming out of a low self-image which we discussed in chapter 1.

Dependency of human beings on each other and on Jesus is the opposite of "macho." This dependency is the healthy kind, because it recognizes just how much we are in need of God and other people for our daily support. It is the knowledge that we can't go it alone. Again, because of culturally learned behavior, this is often harder for boys than for girls.

Religion for Women Only?

This concern about being dependent is also the reason why some people have associated religion principally with women. Being "religious" seemed to imply passivity and living chiefly on the feeling level. The letter to the Galatians lists the fruits of the Holy Spirit as *love, joy, peace, patience, kindness, goodness, faithfulness, humility, and self-control* (Galatians 5:22-23). These qualities have mistakenly been considered somewhat feminine. But that's not the picture that comes across if the whole letter is read. Saint Paul is really saying that these are characteristics *any* true Christian, male or female, should have, along with a very strong and enduring love. The intrepid Paul, who suffered so much for the faith and eventually was martyred, could preach nothing but a very rugged Christianity.

Real Strength

Real strength is often found in what on the surface appears to be weak. For instance, it takes more strength to be gentle and polite with a rude customer than it does to get angry with them. It takes more strength to be on a team and let your teammates "star" than to keep the spotlight on yourself. It takes strength of character to know an answer in class and let somebody else enjoy the success of responding.

This paradox of real strength looking like weakness is well described by the ancient philosopher Lao Tsu:

Yield and overcome;
Bend and be straight;
Empty and be full;
Wear out and be new;
Have little and gain;
Have much and be confused.
Therefore wise men embrace the one
And set an example to all.
Not putting on a display,
They shine forth.
Not justifying themselves,
They are distinguished.
Not boasting,
They receive recognition . . . .

(22, *Tao Te Ching)*

Worth and Achievement

Another challenge is to be able to answer the question: What is a person worth? This is difficult because we have another misplaced linkage to deal with. We find it hard to appreciate the value of a person in and of himself or herself. We keep trying to bring in the productivity or at least the potential of the person. We always link the person and achievement. Thomas Merton speaks about this in his book *No Man Is an Island:*

"It is useless to try to make peace with ourselves by being pleased with everything we have done. In order to settle down in the quiet of our own being we must learn to be detached from the results of our own activity. We must withdraw ourselves, to some extent, from effects that are beyond our control and be content with the good will and the work that are the quiet expression of our inner life. We must be content to live without watching ourselves live, to work without expecting an immediate reward, to love without an instantaneous satisfaction, and to exist without any special recognition."

It's an interesting paradox that if we can be detached from the results of our efforts we have more energy for the task itself. We aren't using all our energy on getting results. And this often means better results!

Being Your Own Person

One of the biggest challenges of the teen years is the resolving of the tension between wanting to be your own person and wanting to be accepted by others — especially those of your own age group. How many fail in this. They live their lives trying to conform to the opinions of others. In teenage terms this is called going along with the crowd or giving in to peer pressures. Many kids do give in. That's sad, because they miss discovering their own unique goodness and talents.

Commitment

Commitment is the name of another challenge. Many people today want to avoid being pinned down about anything. They want to be casual about everything in life. This lack of commitment, while permeating the entire culture, is especially noticeable among youth. How many kids do you know who, having made a promise to do something or go somewhere, will break the original promise? It's as if they had written in an exception clause: "I'll do this if something better doesn't come along" or "if it doesn't get too boring or too hard." In some teenage circles this is the accepted way of acting.

Lack of Commitment

There's no doubt that a lack of commitment in these years is a poor preparation for later life. More importantly, it's wrong even now. It doesn't treat human beings in a way that they are worthy of being treated. It cheapens friendships and can erode relationships. Even William Shakespeare, who wrote so many years ago, was aware of this wrong when he wrote Sonnet 116.

Let me not to the marriage of true minds
Admit impediments. Love is not love
Which alters when it alteration finds,
Or bends with the remover to remove.
O, no, it is an ever-fixed mark
That looks on tempests and is never shaken;
It is the star to every wand'ring bark,
Whose worth's unknown,
    although his height be taken.
Love's not Time's fool,
    though rosy lips and cheeks
Within his bending sickle's compass come.
Love alters not with his brief hours
    and weeks,

But bears it out even to the edge of doom.
If this be error and upon me proved,
I never writ, nor no man ever loved.

Family Life

A forgotten area of commitment is a person's own family. As a young person matures he or she is well aware of the changes taking place within himself or herself. Also, there's the realization that other young people of both sexes are now viewed in a different way. This necessitates the establishment of new relationships. That's all well and good, but meanwhile a young person can forget that important shifts are also taking place within one's own family.

In a family a child's needs and undeveloped skills necessarily put the little one on the receiving end most of the time. That's as it should be. But when a young person reaches the teens he or she should be old enough to be on the giving end at times. At least there should be present the readiness to take on some of the responsibilities of family life.

Your parents will always be your parents. You will always be son or daughter to them. But the adult-child relationship should begin changing. This can be somewhat confusing for all concerned. Still, it's well worth working at, because the final result can be an extremely satisfying friendship with those two special people you call "Mom" and "Dad."

Nearest Neighbor

For these important family relationships to develop something obvious has to happen:

contact must be maintained. Teenagers sometimes forget that, like themselves, their parents are also people in need of continued love and support. To have their teenage children all but vanish during four years of high school and/or four years of college is just not fair to them. And yet the youth subculture encourages this type of thing. When Jesus tells us that his chief commandment is to love both God and our neighbor, we should realize that the word "neighbor" refers first of all to those who are nearest. Who is nearer to you than your family? Jesus never mentioned taking a vacation from loving your family for four or eight years.

The Challenge of Sexuality

Christians and many other peoples have always associated genital sexuality with deep commitment. This type of sexual relationship is so physical and psychologically intimate that it should be marked by care and trust and lasting fidelity. Genital sexuality solely for physical pleasure or to gain popularity or to boost one's ego lacks this necessary dimension of commitment. It turns the experience into something that can only mean unhappiness. On the other hand, a person who treasures the gift of sexuality will, when the right time comes, be able to share this gift with the loved one with a sense of great joy. Such are the rewards of deep commitment.

Listening

One final aspect of being faithful to people is the self-discipline required for good listening. When we discussed how to pray, we talked about listening as the more important part of communication. Father Vincent Dwyer, a Trappist monk, spoke about this at a recent Youth Congress. He remarked that in our age the greatest penance or asceticism is not to say long prayers or to fast from eating food but, rather, to listen well and attentively to other people.

Heaven or Hell

Life is full of many challenges. We can either face these challenges or do everything we can to avoid them. If we choose the latter option we will become people turned in upon ourselves. There are some reputable theologians who claim that such a self-inturning is nothing less than hell itself.

But if we face the challenges of life bravely, give them our very best efforts, then our world will continue to open wider to broader and broader vistas. Our relationships with the Lord and with our fellow human beings will be so deep and so rich that they will even now be a foretaste of heaven.

Spiritual Exercises

1. Looking at personal strengths, like patience, kindness, and self-control, write down your greatest gift along these lines. Then write a note to the Holy Spirit, describing the last time you used this gift and the good that most probably resulted from it.

2. Being faithful to yourself means striving to follow your best gifts and instincts. A great psychologist, Abraham Maslow, wrote: "If you deliberately plan to be less than you are capable of being, then I warn you that you'll be

unhappy for the rest of your life." As honestly and probingly as possible, write down what being faithful to yourself will entail in your life as an adult.

3. A key part of being faithful to the people in your life comes down to really *listening* to them. Write the name of one person, the habit you have that keeps you from listening intently to that person, and what you plan to do about it.

7 / Going Beyond Myself

The teen years are supposed to be a time for discovering oneself, working out what we call an "identity," and seeing oneself as an individual with unique qualities. But there is a danger in this type of self-preoccupation. A person can become so absorbed in oneself that one's vision is extremely narrowed. When that takes place that person's view of life doesn't correspond to the truth. It is too constricted a vision. In reality, it's a big world out there. A lot of things are happening — some good and some bad. And we taste the bittersweet reality of this world according to the number and quality of our involvements in it. It's the only way to live a full life. So, focusing merely on oneself would be life-inhibiting. It would be an unreal and sterile experience — and life is too short for that.

An Antidote for Self-centeredness

Jesus has given us an antidote for this excessive introspection. It's a clear and unmistakeable mandate to care for the poor of this world. The Gospels present Jesus as preferentially associating with the poor and those others on the fringes of society — lepers, sick people, those possessed, prostitutes, and all others rejected by society for one reason or another.

With this in mind, it is interesting to look at the difference in the focus of youth groups in North and South America.

The Latin American View

Latin American youth have no problem seeing in the Gospel Jesus' keen sensitivity and concern for the poor and the outcast. The condemnations the Lord leveled at the rich could hardly be more forcefully expressed. And that *you will always have poor people with you* (Jn 12:8) seems obvious to Latin American young men and women. All they have to do is look around. That's why their church youth groups have chosen as their primary purpose the alleviation of misery and poverty.

Exalted Goals

There is no doubt that the youth of South and Central America feel called to this vital mission. They state it clearly in two recent documents: *Reflexiones Joc 3,* a text of the Young Catholic Workers in Lima, Peru, and *Orientaciones para la Pastoral juvenil en Chile,* written by the National Commission for Youth Ministry in Santiago, Chile. An excerpt from this latter document spells out the exalted goals which should challenge all young Christians in their living of the Gospel message:

- To value everything that is positive and good in this world, no matter where it comes from;
- To foster especially anything that is done for the welfare and betterment of human beings;
- To give oneself wholeheartedly to the building up of the kingdom of God and to oppose prophetically all that is an obstacle to this;

- To discover how to penetrate to the causes of those problems that afflict the people of this world;
- To join forces in the battle for the complete liberation of all enslaved people, a battle against evil itself;
- In a word, we Christian young people accept the Mission given us by the Lord himself: To be the yeast of this world, encouraging and promoting every action that points to peace, equality, justice, and brotherhood . . . .

The North American View

This strong social sense, this kinship with the downtrodden, this outrage over the blatant injustices in modern society is largely missing from corresponding documents of North American youth ministries. Why? Does that mean that the young people of the United States and Canada are naturally less idealistic, less able to give themselves to important causes? Certainly not. But perhaps it does mean that all of us can be formed by the culture we are part of. In a sense we can become victims of that society.

Living in a rich nation, surrounded by affluence, constantly badgered to take up a consumer-oriented, selfish way of life — all these pressures can shape an individual into something less than a complete and willing follower of Christ. It would not be surprising if such a person developed blind spots when certain harsh Gospel statements showed up. How could a person take the following words of Christ literally and still continue to live with a "me-first" attitude toward life?

Jesus looked around at his disciples and said to them, "How hard it will be for rich people to enter the Kingdom of God!"

The disciples were shocked at these words, but Jesus went on to say, "My children, how hard it is to enter the Kingdom of God! It is much harder for a rich person to enter the Kingdom of God than for a camel to go through the eye of a needle" (Mark 10:23-25).

The Sin of Grasping

Michael Warren, a writer and lecturer, remarked that the young people he teaches today at the university are a lot different from those of ten years ago. "If there is any sin or fault which is predominant among them," he said, "it is that of *grasping*." By grasping he meant that their major effort in life is to clutch at, grasp at material goods or worldly success. They appear willing to do anything "to get ahead" economically.

The turbulence of the 1960s brought to the surface a number of major problems, such as racial unrest, civil rights confrontations, and the protests of the "peaceniks." But at least the restless youth of a decade ago had a much less materialistic attitude than that which exists today. In this respect the "flower children" were closer to the Gospel teaching than today's youth. It is tragic that this anti-materialism was so short-lived and that we have returned to a selfish consumerism.

Today we realize that we live in a global village which is economically controlled by multimillion-dollar corporations. Some of these corporations put economic advantage over human rights and basic Christian principles of justice. Many of the world's poor suffer greatly in these capitalistic quicksands. The harder they struggle the deeper they sink. It's time that all of us take a look at the world we are living in. After all, it's *our* world. Christ said he was not going to remove us from this world, but he was going to ask us to do everything we could to transform it. Where injustice exists God's kingdom is not present.

Responsibility or Indifference

Archie Bunker in *All in the Family* once remarked: "Oh, don't worry about him, he's a good Catholic, he don't do nothing about it" (January 15, 1973). Consider the tragedy in this statement. At this point, the temptation might come to a young person to ask: Why has the older generation failed to act? Why have they allowed all these injustices in the world? But that would be a cop-out. What are *you* doing about it? Just because you are young doesn't mean that you can shirk your responsibility in this matter. Father Daniel Berrigan says that the opposite of love is not hatred; it is indifference.

Sins of commission are wrong actions that we do. Sins of omission are good actions that we fail to do. Sins of submission mean going along with cultural trends or with what everyone else is doing in order to remain comfortable and not "rock the boat."

It isn't pleasant to consider all the suffering in the world that is caused by man's greed, prejudice, and injustice. But if we are to be true followers of Christ we have to come to grips with this reality and do what we can to change things.

Personal Suffering

Another reality that we are reluctant to face is personal suffering. The dawn of the teen years means saying farewell to the relatively blissful days of childhood. Not that children don't suffer — they do. But it's only when maturity begins that a person makes a conscious effort to grapple with the profound mystery of human suffering. There are "growing pains" in the movement toward adulthood — not necessarily physical hurts but emotional and psychological stresses which sometimes mean intense personal suffering. Here is a poem by a thirteen-year-old boy which brings this out:

How I Feel

I feel like the sun when it stops shining,
the moon when it goes in.
A boy who has lost his dog, or a girl
that lost her family.

I feel like a chair that has no legs,
a song that has no name, or a bank
that has no money.

I feel like a lamp that has no lightbulb,
a picture that has no meaning,
but most of all I feel pain.

– *Mark Ferreira*

Since all of life is continuous growth, the possibility of suffering will always be nearby.

Hence the need for some understanding or way of looking at this experience which is so much a part of every human life.

The Mystery of Suffering

There are lots of things said about suffering — some helpful and some not. Suffering is not a problem to be solved. It's not a question to be answered. It's a mystery. A person cannot come up with a one-to-one solution to suffering nor a detailed answer that "explains" what is happening. Nonetheless, there are approaches which can help us to cope with this mystery. For one thing, our Christian faith can be a source of comfort. Jesus has promised to respond to our requests for help. There are many helpful texts in the New Testament. As an example, two are quoted here:

My brothers, consider yourselves fortunate when all kinds of trials come your way, for you know that when your faith succeeds in facing such trials, the result is the ability to endure. Make sure that your endurance carries you all the way without failing, so that you may be perfect and complete, lacking nothing (James 1:2-4).

Let us give thanks to the God and Father of our Lord Jesus Christ, the merciful Father, the God from whom all help comes! He helps us in all our troubles, so that we are able to help others who have all kinds of troubles, using the same help that we ourselves have received from God. Just as we have a share in Christ's many sufferings, so also through Christ we share in God's great help. If we suffer, it is for your help

INR

and salvation; if we are helped, then you too are helped and given the strength to endure with patience the same sufferings that we also endure. So our hope in you is never shaken; we know that just as you share in our sufferings, you also share in the help we receive (2 Corinthians 1:3-7).

There is also much insight into human suffering which can be found in literature. Note the wisdom in this little poem by Robert Browning Hamilton:

I walked a mile with Pleasure,
She chattered all the way;
But left me none the wiser
For all she had to say.

I walked a mile with Sorrow,
And ne'er a word said she;
But, oh, the things I learned from her
When Sorrow walked with me!

Reflections on Suffering

Here are a few further reflections on suffering which you might find helpful from *Good News from Matthew:*

1. Does God actually send certain sufferings to certain people? Does he plot our misery? Some people may think so, because of early childhood experiences or because of remarks by parents and teachers. But such a concept does not square with what Jesus has revealed. The God whom Jesus revealed is Love itself. A loving father never sends deliberate misery. We suffer both in mind and body because of the vulnerability of the human condition (that is, because of original sin).

We certainly do not suffer because God likes to see us in pain.

2. Do we suffer in this life for our sins? The answer to this question is both yes and no. We do not suffer for our sins in the way the ancient Jews thought. For example, when the ancient Jews were struck by famine, they would interpret the disaster as a punishment from God for misbehavior. This primitive way of thinking was too simple; God does not act in that way. To put it in more concrete terms, God doesn't see to it that we stub our toe after we've said a swear word. We do suffer in this life for our sins, however, in the sense that sin and unkindness have their own way of bringing misery into our lives. The saying is true that we begin our heaven or hell here on earth.

3. Of what value is human suffering? This question can be approached from many angles. The value does not lie in the suffering itself but in the attitude with which we approach it. Two axioms apply here. The first axiom is: When we pray to be delivered from suffering, God often changes us rather than the situation. The second axiom is that outstanding piece of advice: ". . . to accept what I must, change what I can, and have the wisdom to know the difference."

Of course, the highest value of human suffering is that of serving the good of another human being. Jesus' own death for us is a witness to that.

4. Is there any value to self-imposed suffering (self-discipline)? Self-discipline is of no value in itself. But it has value to the extent that it helps bear unavoidable pain maturely.

Talk to a Friend

Probably the most important thing to do when suffering enters your life is not to keep everything locked within yourself but, rather, to talk it out with a friend. Maybe the other person can't solve your problem (after all, suffering is not a problem to be solved but a mystery to be lived), but it does help you to get the problem out in the open. This will at least give you some perspective on it and perhaps a little good advice besides. The support and encouragement of friends is necessary when times are tough. If we don't talk to a trusted somebody, we usually stay confused or upset or more depressed for a longer period of time. Remember also what was said about prayer in chapter 3. Why should we hesitate to pour out our heart to Jesus himself and to trust in his personal love for each one of us?

Spiritual Exercises

1. Reread the list of goals for young Christians on pages 74-75. Privately, or with a small group, use this list to draw up one of your own. Type or print your goals on good paper and keep it where you will notice it often.

2. Divide a sheet of paper into two columns: A — The unpleasant things in my life that I must accept; B — The unpleasant things in my life that I can change. List one thing in each column. Then write a letter to Jesus, telling him your thoughts and feelings about the things you listed.

3. Giant corporations control much of our national economy. More than we like to think, they also influence our thinking and desires. If you want to be more your own person and to help our society become more just, write to the following address for a list of companies with unjust practices whose products can be boycotted:

Interfaith Center on Corporate Responsibility
475 Riverside Drive — Room 566
New York, NY 10027.

TAIZÉ

8 / Taizé: A Report from France

We arrived in Taizé late in the evening. At once we saw the buses from all over Europe unloading their travel-weary but happy passengers, most of them with knapsacks in tow. Immediately, despite the many language barriers, everyone's friendliness impressed us. Proceeding to the welcome tent marked "English" we were met by a young Dutchman who showed us to our lodgings and told us about the schedule.

The Brothers of Taizé

Taizé is a tiny village in the southeast of France. It is the birthplace of the community of the Brothers of Taizé, who now number eighty members throughout the world. Brother Roger came to Taizé alone in 1940. In 1949 seven Brothers professed their vows to celibacy and the common life. The Brothers of Taizé are now an Ecumenical Community which welcomes Protestants and, since 1969, Roman Catholic members. The Brothers root their life in God, yet remain keenly aware of suffering humanity in need of reconciliation. This double emphasis of contemplation and the social struggle is one of the features of the community which has attracted youth. The Brothers lived in relative isolation for the first twenty years of their existence. Gradually, young people in Europe were attracted by their witness of community, authenticity, and deep prayer.

The Council of Youth

The number of youth visiting Taizé grew larger and larger until the Easter of 1970. At that time Brother Roger saw the need of organizing this large group, so he announced the formation of a Council of Youth. The interior or spiritual preparation of the Council of Youth lasted four and a half years. Themes were explored each year relating to the "inner adventure" in preparation for the "public adventure." At the end of this process 40,000 young people from 100 different countries gathered at Taizé in late summer 1974. Today the Council of Youth is active on a worldwide basis.

The Life of Prayer

It was the life of prayer at Taizé which most impressed visitors. The Brothers now at Taizé meet three times each day for common prayer. Their church seems to provide the perfect environment for silence and contemplation. The long shadows and the faint flickering light coming from the many candles adorning the front altar invite one to prayer. The floor of the church is entirely carpeted and there are no pews. The Brothers, who don simple white habits for common prayer, sit along the center of the church and the youth huddle beside them on the floor. A sense of reverence and presence permeates the air. Psalms and Scripture readings comprise the office which is recited in various languages, such as English, Bengali, French, or Chinese, depending on the nationalities of the guests in attendance. There are times for silence and deep

SHOP

meditation. Hymns and refrains are sung by all. Intercessory prayers for suffering humanity pour forth from many lips. Finally, there's a poignant closing prayer by Brother Roger which speaks to the deepest longings of the human heart.

Silence and Prayer

In addition to this large church there is a crypt church beneath it and a Roman church in the village. Both of these serve as places for young people to dwell in contemplative prayer. These two churches are also carpeted and dimly lit and very conducive to meditation. The people in the village open up their homes and provide lodgings where young people may stay and live in complete silence for extended periods of time.

When a person arrives at Taizé he or she is expected to participate in one of two ways: either in silence or in dialogue with others. The latter option works this way: The groups meet three times a day and pray together, sharing their faith experiences with each other and praising God for his many graces.

The silent option allows the person to live most of the day completely in solitude and prayer. It was this aspect of Taizé that most impressed me. Silence is vital to such an atmosphere. The young people who are spending a week or more in this peaceful silence live in a compound of tents separated from the rest. (Visitors to Taizé live in tents which they rent for a nominal fee. There is also a self-contained food service which is worked by young adults, most of whom are staying for longer periods of time.)

Searching for the Sources

One of the Brothers remarked to us about the youth coming to Taizé today: "They are searching for the sources. They ask: 'Where is the source of existence? How can Christ be the source of our existence?' This is the central question." And yet, while Taizé is a place for both self-discovery and the discovery of God, it is not a movement, not an island unto itself. The Brothers encourage the youth to return to their local situations and parishes. If they find them lifeless, they are to bring to them a spark of the new life which they have discovered at Taizé.

Focus on Christ

While we sat among the 2,000 young worshipers on Pentecost Sunday we were struck by an important fact. Unlike many North American youth gatherings, the focus was on Christ and not so much on the group itself. While group support for contemplative prayer was very evident, Taizé spoke most profoundly to us of the need to encounter Christ and to meet God alone in the deepest center of our own hearts, abandoning our American fear of silence as something empty or boring.

We have spoken of the South American emphasis on social and political action. In North America we find most successful youth retreats focus on developing a better self-image and hence the capacity to be loved and to reach out more in love toward others. At Taizé the primary focus is to go up the mountain alone and meet God, who is the Source of all life, and to come down from the mountain to enter more deeply into the struggles of men and women on this earth.

The Search for God

All of these are important aspects of a sound spirituality and none is the sole answer or approach. What we need to do is to blend this search for God within us with the search for alleviating the sufferings of our brothers and sisters throughout the world. No one can do this for us. We have to do it ourselves.

We concluded our stay in France with a visit to a Trappist monastery which is also frequented by young people. We spoke with a monk there, and we shall conclude with a quotation from him:

"Young people are seeking to find a way of life. It is clear today that we need a deeper sense of life; they come here to find an answer. They seek it through meditation. They have a distaste of life today which doesn't make sense to them. The only answer is to seek God."

Spiritual Exercises

1. Ask your parish priest if there is a contemplative monastery of monks or nuns within driving distance of your home. If there is, write to the monastery to see if you can attend prayer or perhaps even have a tour of the premises. Another interesting place to visit would be a Quaker* meeting. This might be found in the yellow pages of your phone directory under "Churches, Society of Friends." This group is very cordial to visitors and would be happy to have you attend.

2. If you would like more information about Taizé you can write for the *Letter from Taizé*, the special issue in July-August 1979. This booklet of 35 pages is very readable and contains photographs. One copy costs five French francs, postage included. For payment, go to a bank and ask that a bank check be drawn in French francs and payable at a French bank. Send your name and address with the check to: *Letter from Taizé,* F-71250 Taizé-Communaute, France.

* The Quakers are a beautiful, peaceful group of people founded by George Fox (a contemplative — "hippie") in England in 1647. Their worship consists in sitting together in silence for 60 minutes. Silence is very important to Quakers to nourish their spiritual life. "Inner Light" is the expression they use to describe God's presence in each person.

Conclusion

The subtitle of this book is *A Spiritual Guide for Young Adults*. We would like to make one final comment and it has to do with the adjective "spiritual." Some people think that anything spiritual would be only a part of a person, that it would be unrelated to a person's whole humanity. That's not true. In fact, a very good definition of spirituality is a personal relationship with Jesus, the God-man.

Unless we acknowledge Jesus as a true man, a full-fledged member of the human race, then our approach to God could encounter all sorts of difficulties. The way to the Father is Jesus and him alone. Also, it's a comfort to know that we have a Savior who understands us perfectly. He was at one time a young adult. He's been through it. When we talk to him in our prayers he knows what we are talking about.

Perhaps the most important thing to realize is that a relationship with God *is possible*. It's not something only of the distant past. It's not something reserved to priests, Brothers, or nuns. Nor is it meant only for holy people, or even for adults only. It's a possibility for you here and now. It may sound too good to be true — but it's true nonetheless: *You can get in touch with Jesus*! Why don't you?

Recommended Books

The following inexpensive paperback books can be ordered from local religious bookstores or directly from Liguori Publications.

Love Yourself by Edward Richardson, M.M., $1.50

How to Develop a Better Self-image by Russell M. Abata, C.SS.R., $2.25

To Love and Be Loved by John C. Tormey, $1.50

Good News from Matthew by Joseph Moore, $1.95

How to Read and Pray the Gospels by Marilyn Norquist, $1.50

The Beatitudes: Jesus' Pattern for a Happy Life by Marilyn Norquist, $2.95

Contemplative Prayer by James Borst, M.H.M., $1.50